MEDICARE, You Earned This!

A Practical Guide for Medicare Beneficiaries

Toby Stark

Printed in the United States of America
Published in Hellertown, PA
Cover and interior design by Anna Magruder
Library of Congress Control Number 2025928240
ISBN 979-8-89420-083-5
For more information or to place bulk orders, contact the author or the publisher at Jennifer@BrightCommunications.net.

To the Eatontown Lions Club "We Serve"

Contents

Introduction: Welcome to Medicare!

Medicare is one of the most important benefits that you can pay for and earn. It is a healthcare financial safety net for people 65 years and older. (Some younger people with disabilities who are on Social Security also qualify for Medicare.)

There is so much misinformation leading up to your enrollment into Medicare, compounded likely by your disdain of medical insurance to start with. You have been with your employer for many years and probably just renewed your medical insurance as is, never bothering to understand the benefits you had. But after your retirement, you leave the safe employer-sponsored plan. You are thrown out to the wolves, left alone to decide what is best for you with no education and no motivation to learn.

Turning 65? Time to Unlock Your Medicare Superpowers!
First off, congratulations! Hitting 65 is a major milestone, and with it comes a special perk: Medicare. But let's be honest, navigating Medicare can feel like trying to assemble furniture without the instructions. Between confusing terms, deadlines, and plan choices—where do you even start?

That's where this book comes in. Think of it as your Medicare GPS—giving you clear directions, steering you around the potholes (like late penalties!), and helping you find the best route for your health and wallet.

If you're feeling a little overwhelmed, don't worry, you're not alone! Medicare can seem confusing at first, but this book is here to guide you every step of the way.

In the next few chapters, we'll break Medicare down into simple, easy-to-understand sections. Whether you're wondering when to enroll, which plan to choose, or how much it will cost, we've got you covered.

What's in It for You?

By the time you finish this book, you will:

- ✓ Understand Medicare in plain English—no insurance jargon here!
- ✓ Know exactly when and how to enroll—and how to avoid costly mistakes.
- ✓ Confidently choose between Original Medicare, Medicare Advantage, and Medigap.
- ✓ Learn what's covered, what's not, and how to fill in the gaps.
- ✓ Be able to navigate costs, prescription drug plans, and extra benefits.
- ✓ Get tips on keeping your healthcare costs low while maximizing your benefits.

Why This Book?

Medicare isn't one-size-fits-all. Your health needs, budget, and lifestyle all play a role in which plan is best for you.

You probably didn't wake up thinking, *Wow, I can't wait to read about Medicare today!* (If you did, you might be the first!) But here's the thing—making the right Medicare decisions now can save you thousands of dollars and ensure you get the best healthcare possible.

Unfortunately, most Medicare guides feel like they were written by robots for robots. This book is different. It's clear, to the point, and (dare I say it?) even a little fun.

How to Use This Book

Each chapter is designed to give you the most important information in a way that's easy to follow, with real-life examples, checklists, and quick summaries so you can find what you need fast. Whether you want to read cover to cover or just skip to the parts that matter most at the time, it's all here.

Ready to take control of your Medicare choices? Let's get started!

Chapter 1: Medicare Basics:
What You Need to Know

Medicare: It's the healthcare program everyone needs at 65, but no one really understands. And that's okay! Let's break it down into bite-sized pieces so you can make sense of it without needing a Ph.D. in insurance.

What Is Medicare, Anyway?

Medicare is a government health insurance program primarily for people 65 and older (though some younger people with disabilities also qualify). It helps pay for hospital stays, doctor visits, and even prescription drugs. But Medicare is not one-size-fits-all. In fact, Medicare comes in multiple "parts," each covering specific services. Choosing the right part is the first step to getting the coverage you need.

The Four Parts of Medicare—Explained in 30 Seconds

Medicare Part A: Think of this as hospital coverage. It helps pay for hospital stays, skilled nursing care, and some home healthcare.

Medicare Part B: This covers doctor visits, outpatient services, preventive care, and medical services like X-rays, lab tests, and medical equipment, such as wheelchairs, blood sugar monitors, and lancets.

Parts A and B together are often called Original Medicare.

Medicare Part C (Medicare Advantage): This is a private insurance alternative that bundles Parts A and B together—often with extras like vision, dental, and prescription drug coverage.

💊 **Medicare Part D:** This is your prescription drug plan, helping cover the cost of medications.

Who's Eligible for Medicare?

If you're 65 (Or about to be. We'll talk about the initial enrollment period in chapter 3), you're likely eligible, especially if you or your spouse worked and paid Medicare taxes for at least 10 years. If you're already getting Social Security benefits, you would have been automatically enrolled in Parts A and B. If you're not yet getting Social Security benefits, you'll need to sign up during your Initial Enrollment Period. (More on that soon!)

My Medicare Action Plan: Quick Checklist

Before moving on to the next chapter, take a moment to check due to my enrollment in social security, off these steps:

☐ Do I qualify for Medicare at 65? Am I automatically enrolled due to my enrollment in social security, or do I need to sign up?

☐ Do I understand the differences between Parts A, B, C, and D?

☐ What type of coverage do I think I'll need?

Next Up: Choosing the Right Medicare Plan for YOU

Now that you know the basics, the next step is figuring out which Medicare path is best for your health, lifestyle, and budget. In the next chapter, we'll compare your options side by side—so you can make the smartest choice without all the stress.

Chapter 2: Medicare Parts A, B, C, and D—Demystified

You've heard of the alphabet soup that is Medicare: Parts A, B, C, and D. We talked about the basics in Chapter 1. But what do they really mean—and how do they work together? Let's break it all down further in a way that makes sense, even if you've never cracked open a healthcare brochure.

🛏 Part A: Hospital Insurance

Think of Part A as your hospital safety net. If you end up admitted to a hospital or need skilled nursing care, this part kicks in. Most people get Part A for *free* because they (or their spouse) paid Medicare taxes while working for at least 10 years.

What's covered:

- Hospital stays*
- Skilled nursing facility care after a hospital stay
- Hospice care
- Some home health services like physical, occupational, and speech therapy.

What's not:

- Long-term care (nursing home stays)
- Doctor visits (That's Part B!)

* **Costs:** You'll pay a deductible for each hospital stay, so it's not *entirely* free.

🩺 Part B: Medical Insurance

Part B is your everyday health coverage. This is your go-to for regular checkups and treatments, including doctor visits, outpatient care, and preventive services like flu shots. Unlike Part A, Part B is *not* free, even if you (or your spouse) worked and paid Medicare taxes for more than 10 years. Most people pay a standard monthly premium for Part B, and there's also a deductible. Premium example $202 and deductible example $285 year.

What's covered:

- Doctor visits (any doctor that accepts Medicare)
- Lab tests and X-rays
- Preventive care like cancer screenings
- Outpatient care and home health services
- Durable medical equipment such as wheelchairs and walkers

What's not covered: [Dental and Vision coverage. Hearing Care, long-term care, cosmetic surgery, prescription drugs, routing care (physical)].

Parts A and B together are called Original Medicare.

Part C: Medicare Advantage

This is where Medicare gets a makeover. Medicare Advantage plans (Part C) are offered by private insurance companies. You might have premiums, but there are a lot of plans that offer $0 premium plans. Most plans have a deductible, co-pays, coinsurance and a maximum out-of-pocket (MOOP).

Medicare Advantage plans combine Parts A and B—often with extra perks like:

- Vision benefits
- Dental benefits
- Gym memberships
- Transportation to doctor visits
- Over-the-counter (OTC) benefits, such as vitamins, toothbrushes, toothpaste, eye care, cold and allergy medications, and pain relief.
- Prescription drug coverage

👍 **Pros** to Medicare Advantage plans:

- They are a one-stop shop.

- Some even have $0 premiums.

Cons to Medicare Advantage plans: You may be limited to provider networks (like an HMO or PPO). And, you have to navigate pre-approvals and prior authorizations before some services are approved.

✏ Part D: Prescription Drug Coverage

Medicare Part D helps you pay for prescription medications. Plans are offered by private insurers, and they vary in cost and coverage.

What to know:

- You can add Part D to Original Medicare (Parts A + B).
- Many Medicare Advantage plans (Part C) already include drug coverage.
- Plans have a list of covered drugs, called a formulary.

Beware: If you don't sign up for Part D when you are first eligible and don't have other creditable drug coverage, you might pay a late penalty.

Medicare Mashups: What You Can Combine

Here's how people typically build their Medicare package:

- **Original Medicare (Parts A + B) + Part D + Medigap** (more on that in Chapter 3)
- **Medicare Advantage plans (Part C)** = All-in-one plan that often includes RX Coverage

✔ My Medicare Action Plan: Know Your Parts

☐ Do I understand what each Medicare part covers?
☐ Am I leaning toward Original Medicare (Parts A + B) or Medicare Advantage (Part C)?
☐ Do I need prescription drug coverage (Part D)?
☐ Am I willing to pay extra for more flexibility, or do I prefer an all-in-one plan?

Next up: The Enrollment Guide

Now that you understand the Parts of Medicare, we'll talk about when and how to sign up to get the coverage that you earned!

Chapter 3: The Enrollment Guide: When and How to Sign Up

Okay, now that you've got the Medicare lingo down, let's talk about *when* and *how* to enroll. Because here's the deal: Timing is everything. If you miss a deadline, you could end up with late penalties or gaps in your coverage. No thanks!

The Key Enrollment Periods

Medicare has five different enrollment periods. Let's break this down into bite-sized chunks.

1. Initial Enrollment Period (IEP)

- **When:** A seven-month window that begins *three months before* the month you turn 65, includes your birthday month, and ends *three months after*.
- **What to do:** Enroll in Medicare Part A and/or Part B. You can also join a Medicare Advantage plan (Part C) or prescription drug plan (Part D).
- **Why it matters:** Missing this window could mean a late enrollment penalty.

2. General Enrollment Period (GEP)

- **When:** Every year from January 1 to March 31.
- **What to do:** Sign up for Part A and/or Part B if you didn't during your IEP. (But not Medicare Advantage plan (Part C) and prescription drug plans (Part D), more on that next.)
- **Heads up:** Coverage starts the first of the month after you enroll, and you *may* pay a late penalty for missing your initial enrollment period.

3. Special Enrollment Period (SEP)

- **When:** If you delayed enrolling in Medicare because you had coverage through an employer (yours or your spouse's).
- **What to do:** You'll have **eight months** after your job-based insurance ends to sign up for Part A and/or Part B.
- Note: For people who work past 65 and qualify to delay Medicare with creditable employer coverage, there is an 8-month Special Enrollment Period that allows you to enroll in Part A (if you haven't yet), Part B, Part C and Part D without late penalties. This Special Enrollment Period is tricky though. Why? Because while you have the whole 8 months to get Parts A & B, you only get the first 2 months to enroll in Part C or Part D without penalty. If you enroll after the two-month mark, you'll face late enrollment penalties for Part D, regardless of whether you end up with a stand-alone Part D plan or a Medicare Advantage plan that includes drug coverage.

4. Medicare Advantage (Part C) and Prescription Drug Plans (Part D) Open Enrollment

- **When:** Every year from October 15 to December 7.
- **What to do:** Join, drop, or switch your Medicare Advantage plan (Part C) or prescription drug plan (Part D).
- **Pro tip:** Even if you're happy with your plan, review it each year because it can change!

5. Medigap Open Enrollment

- **When:** Starts the month you turn 65 and are enrolled in Part B. Lasts for six months.
- **What to do:** Apply for a Medigap (Supplemental) plan without medical underwriting.

- **Why is this the best time?** This is when you're guaranteed acceptance into Medigap, regardless of health.

6. Medicare Advantage Open Enrollment Period (MAOEP)

- **What:** If you are on, an advantage plan, you have the opportunity for a one-time change. The open enrollment period is not open for folks who are enrolled in Part D. Their annual enrollment period ends on 12/7.
- **When:** January 1 to March 31
- **What to do:** During this time, if you are already enrolled in a Medicare Advantage (MA) plan, you can make one change to your coverage. For example, you can switch to a different MA plan or you can leave your MA plan to return to Original Medicare, with or without a Part D prescription drug plan. This period is for existing MA enrollees to make a plan change. It is different from the main Medicare Annual Enrollment Period (AEP).

How to Enroll

There are a few ways to sign up for Medicare, depending on your situation:

- **Automatically enrolled?** If you're already receiving Social Security Part A or Railroad Retirement benefits— you're in! Your Medicare card will arrive in the mail.
- **Need to sign up manually?** Do it online at ssa.gov/Medicare, by phone at 1-800-MEDICARE, or in person at your local Social Security office. Yes, this is where the Medicare beneficiary needs to prove their identity. After all, they are going to be taking advantage of a benefit from the government that we all pay for, so it better BE the right person! Usually what happens is the Social Security Administration runs Medicare. Few people know or understand this. So when they apply

for benefits, they need to be able to log in to their Social Security benefits, portal to verify their identity, then they may proceed with filling out the application. It all takes about 15 minutes.

⬤ Don't Forget!

- If you want a Medicare Advantage plan (Part C) or a prescription drug plan (Part D), you'll enroll through a private insurer.
- If you want to purchase a Medigap plan (Medicare supplemental insurance), they are also purchased through private insurance companies.

☑ My Medicare Action Plan: Enrollment Essentials

☐ When is my Initial Enrollment Period?

☐ Do I qualify for a Special Enrollment Period?

☐ Have I noted the dates for Medicare's open enrollment?

☐ Do I want Original Medicare, Medicare Advantage, or Medigap?

Next Up: Filling in the Gaps!

Now that you have a plan for when and how to enroll, we'll compare Medicare plans to help you decide which one is best for you.

Chapter 4: Comparing Medicare Plans: What's Best for *You*?

Okay, so you've got the basics down. You know your A, B, C, and D. You know when to sign up. Now comes the million-dollar question: **Which Medicare plan should you choose?** This chapter is all about comparing your options—Original Medicare (Part A + B) with Medicare Advantage (Part C) and Medigap, so you can find the combo that fits *you*, not just the fine print.

The Big Two: Original Medicare vs. Medicare Advantage

Feature	Original Medicare (A + B)	Medicare Advantage (Part C)
Provider choice	Any doctor or hospital that accepts Medicare	Usually a network (HMO or PPO)
Referrals needed?	No	Often yes
Includes drug coverage?	No (add Part D separately)	Usually yes
Extras (dental, vision, etc.)	No	Often included
Out-of-pocket limits	No limit	Annual out-of-pocket max limit
Can add Medigap?	Yes	No
Nationwide coverage?	Yes	Usually limited regionally

So Which One Should You Choose?
Go with Original Medicare (Part A + B) if:

- You want freedom to see any doctor or hospital in the United States.
- You don't mind paying for separate drug (Part D) and Medigap plans.
- You travel frequently or split time between states.
- You want fewer plan restrictions.

Try Medicare Advantage (Part C) if:

- You want all-in-one coverage (hospital, doctor, drug plans).
- You're okay with provider networks and referrals.
- You like extra benefits like dental or vision coverage
- You want a low or $0 premium. (But watch those copays!)

Medigap: A Supplemental Safety Net

Medigap, or Medicare Supplement, is coverage offered by insurance carriers to pick up where Medicare leaves off.

Medigap fills the "gaps" in Original Medicare (Part A + Part B)—like copays, deductibles, and coinsurance. Plans are standardized and labeled A through N. But you will mostly focus on two plans G and N.

👍 **Pros:**

- Predictable out-of-pocket costs
- Use any Medicare-accepting doctor
- No referrals required

👎 **Cons:**

- Monthly premiums
- Doesn't cover dental or vision
- Doesn't work with Medicare Advantage plans (Part C)

Best time to buy: Approx 6 months before your birthday month. If you miss that you still have your six-month Medigap

Open Enrollment, which starts when you turn 65 and enroll in Part B.

Real-Life Scenarios

Sharon lives in two states throughout the year. She chooses Original Medicare + Medigap for freedom to see doctors anywhere.

Bob wants dental and vision, doesn't travel, and loves his local clinic. He goes with a Medicare Advantage plan that covers all his needs with a $0 premium.

☑ My Medicare Action Plan: Pick Your Path

☐ Do I want flexibility or convenience?
☐ Do I need extra benefits like dental or vision?
☐ Do I travel or live in more than one state?
☐ Do I prefer predictable costs or low premiums?

Next Up: Filling in the Gaps

Chapter 5: Medigap 101: Filling in the Gaps (The Supplemental Scoop You Need!)

So you've got Original Medicare (Part A + B), and you're thinking:

This covers everything I need, right?
Well … a*lmost.*
That's where Medigap comes in. Medigap (a.k.a. Medicare Supplement Insurance) helps cover the costs that Original Medicare doesn't—like copayments, coinsurance, and deductibles. In other words, it helps fill in the gaps.

What Exactly Is Medigap?

- **Private insurance** you buy in addition to Original Medicare (Part A + B). (You must have Parts A and B to buy it.)
- Helps with out-of-pocket costs *after* Medicare pays its share.
- Doesn't work with Medicare Advantage plans (Part C).
- As mentioned before, plans range from A through N. However, plans G and N are the most common. (More on this next.)

Why You Might Want Medigap

Type of Expense	Without Medigap	With Medigap Plan G
Part A hospital deductible	$1,736 (2026)	✅ Covered
Part B deductible	$283 (2026)	❌ You pay it
20% of	❌ Not covered	✅ Covered
Annual out-of-pocket max	❌ None	✅ Predictable

Medigap Plans: The ABCs (Actually A–N)

In most states, there are **10 standardized plans,** each with different levels of coverage. The most popular are plans G and N—and sometimes F.

Plan G

- Most comprehensive for new enrollees
- Covers everything except the Part B deductible
- Great if you want peace of mind and predictability

Plan N

- Lower premiums than Plan G
- Small copays at the doctor ($20) or ER ($50)
- Doesn't cover excess charges if a provider does not agree to the Medicare fee schedule. (This is rare, but possible.)

Plan F

- Covers everything—yes, even the Part B deductible!
- This is only available for people who were eligible for Medicare before January 1, 2020. It's not available to new Medicare folks.

Medigap Made Simple – Comparison Chart

Benefit	Plan G	Plan N
Part A hospital coinsurance	✓	✓
Part B coinsurance	✓	✓ *
Blood (first three pints)	✓	✓
Hospice coinsurance	✓	✓
Skilled nursing facility	✓	✓
Part A deductible	✓	✓
Part B deductible	✗	✗
Part B excess charges	✓	✗
Foreign travel emergency	✓	✓

Plan N includes copays: up to $20 for doctor visits and $50 for ER.

Real-Life Scenarios
Joe: The Snowbird
Joe spends half the year in Arizona and the other half in Minnesota. He wants to see doctors anywhere, anytime. He chooses Original Medicare + Medigap Plan G, so he's covered coast to coast—with no surprise bills.
Linda: Budget-Savvy Grandma
Linda's in good health and watches her spending. She picks Plan N for a lower premium and doesn't mind the occasional small copay. She avoids doctors who charge excess fees and pockets the savings. ***When Should You Buy a Medigap Plan?***

The golden window is your **Medigap Open Enrollment Period**:

- Begins the first month you're 65 and enrolled in Part B
- Lasts for six months
- You're guaranteed to be accepted, regardless of health.
- After that? Insurance companies can deny coverage or charge more.

🛒 How to Shop for a Medigap Plan

Plans are standardized. Plan G is the same no matter who sells it. The only differences? Price and customer service.

Insurance Company	Monthly Premium (Plan G)	Ratings
Company A	$128 per month	☆☆☆☆☆
Company B	$145 per month	☆☆☆☆
Company C	$119 per month	☆☆☆☆

🛒 Shop around! Use Medicare's plan finder or speak with a trusted broker.

🚫 What Medigap Doesn't Cover

- Long-term care (nursing homes)
- Vision or dental services
- Hearing aids
- Prescription drugs (You'll need Part D!)

✅ My Medicare Action Plan: Medigap Checklist

☐ Do I have Original Medicare (Part A + B)?
☐ Am I within my six-month Medigap enrollment window?
☐ Do I prefer predictable out-of-pocket costs?
☐ Have I compared prices from different companies?
☐ Do I want Plan G, Plan N, or another option?

Chapter 6: Medicare Costs

Let's talk money. Although Medicare helps cover many healthcare expenses, it's not free. Understanding what you'll actually pay can save you from costly surprises down the road. Here's your Medicare money map—clear, simple, and sprinkled with a few pro tips.

Part A: Hospital Insurance

Premiums: Most people don't pay a premium. If you (or your spouse) worked and paid Medicare taxes into the program for at least 10 years, Part A is premium-free.

Other costs: You still have out-of-pocket costs. For example:

Service	Your Cost (2026)
Monthly premium	$0 (if you qualify)
Hospital deductible	$1,736 per benefit period* (approx.)
Hospital stay days 1–60	$0 per day
Hospital stay days 61–90	$434 per day (approx.)
Hospital stay days 91+ (lifetime reserve)	$868 per day (approx.) (up to 60 days lifetime)

* A "benefit period" resets after 60 days out of the hospital—not just once a year!

Part B: Medical Insurance

Premium: You *do* pay a monthly premium—and possibly more, depending on your income. The base monthly premium is $185. This is for 2025. 2026 is proposed to be $202.90

Other costs: You'll also have to meet an annual deductible and pay coinsurances.

Type of Cost	Your Cost
Monthly premium	$202.90
Annual deductible	$257 approx. $283 in 2026
Coinsurance	20% of approved costs after deductible

Income related monthly adjustment amount: If you earn more, you might pay more (called IRMAA). This is additional premium you have to pay to Medicare.

Tip: If your income has decreased due to a life-changing event (e.g., retirement), you can request a review of your Medicare premiums by submitting Form SSA-44 to the Social Security Administration. Just type it in your search engine to download the form.

Medicare Advantage (Part C)

Instead of paying for Parts A, B, and D separately, Medicare Advantage (Part C) bundles it all—but costs still vary.

Premium: These vary widely.

Other costs: These also vary widely.

Type of Cost	What You Might Pay
Monthly premium	$0–$100+ (varies widely)
Deductibles and copays	Vary by plan
Max out-of-pocket (MOOP)	Up to $9,200/year (in-network, 2026)

Bonus: Some plans include dental, vision, gym memberships, and more.

Part D: Prescription Drug Coverage

Premium: They vary by plan. The average is around $50.

Other costs: Costs vary depending on the plan you choose. Here's the typical breakdown:

Type of Cost	What You Might Pay
Monthly premium	Varies by plan (average ~$50)
Annual deductible	Up to $615 (Some plans waive this, and it changes every year)
Copays/ coinsurance	Varies by tier and drug
Coverage gap (a.k.a. Donut Hole)	Has been eliminated and now the max spend will be $2,000, $2,100 for 2026.

Pro Tip: Use Medicare's Plan Finder at Medicare.gov to compare drug prices and save big or ask your independent insurance broker for assistance. This is a service they should assist you with.

Comparing Monthly Costs: A Snapshot

Plan Type	Monthly Premium	Other Costs
Original Medicare (A + B)	$202	Deductibles, 20% coinsurance
+ Medigap Plan G	$100–$300	Covers most cost gaps
+ Part D Drug Plan	Average $35	Prescription copays/ coinsurance
Medicare Advantage	$0–$100+	Copays, max out-of-pocket limit

Real-Life Scenarios
Susan: Predictable Planner

Susan wants to know exactly what she'll pay each month. She chooses Original Medicare (Part A + B), Medigap Plan G, and a low-cost prescription drug plan (Part D). Her total premium is about $320 per month, but she rarely pays more than a few dollars at the doctor.

Tom: The Bargain Hunter

Tom picks a $0-premium Medicare Advantage plan (Part C) with built-in drug coverage. He saves on premiums, but he pays copays when he visits the doctor. It works great—until an unexpected hospital stay sets him back $2,500.

☑ My Medicare Action Plan: Money Checklist

☐ Do I qualify for free Part A?

☐ What's my Part B premium based on my income?

☐ Have I estimated my total out-of-pocket costs (not just premiums)?

☐ Would I prefer predictable monthly costs or lower up front and more if/when I need care?

☐ Have I shopped around for the best value?

Chapter 7: Medicare Part D: Prescription Drug Plans

Medicare Part D provides prescription drug coverage. These plans are available through private insurance companies that have been approved by Medicare. You can obtain Part D coverage in two ways, depending on your plan.

1. **Original Medicare (Part A or Part B):** If you have Original Medicare, you are entitled to benefits under Part A, or you can be enrolled in Part B. You also qualify to purchase the Standalone Part D Plan.
2. **Medicare Advantage Plan (Part C):** If you have Medicare Advantage, your plan might include prescription drug coverage.

It's important to enroll in a prescription drug plan (Part D) when you're first eligible for Medicare to avoid a permanent late enrollment penalty. The only exception is if you have other creditable prescription drug coverage, such as through your job.

- **Penalty**: The penalty will be 1% of the national base beneficiary premium multiplied by the number of full months you were without coverage.
- **Duration**: This penalty is added to your monthly premium for as long as you have Part D coverage. If you waited to enroll for one year, you would pay a 10% penalty on the national average RX plan, which is $36.78 so you would have to pay $3.67 added to your premium every month for the rest of your life or as long as you are enrolled in Medicare. Think about if

you waited even longer! So it is 1% a month or a max of 10% a year if you wait to enroll in a RX plan and are deemed a late enrollee.

Anatomy of a Part D Plan: What You Pay in 2026

In 2026, Medicare Part D plans have a simplified structure with a $2,000 annual out-of-pocket cap, eliminating the previous "donut hole" coverage gap. Here's how costs break down:

Stage	What You Pay (2026)
Deductible	Up to $615 (varies by plan)*
Initial coverage	Copays/coinsurance based on drug tier
Out-of-pocket maximum	$2,100 annually; after reaching this, you pay $0

Although the cap is indexed so it may increase every year Some plans may offer a $0 deductible, but this varies.*

Drug Tiers: Understanding Costs

Drugs in Part D plans are categorized into tiers, affecting your out-of-pocket costs.

Tier	Drug Type	Estimated Cost Range
Tier 1	Preferred generics	$0–$5
Tier 2	Other generic drugs	$5–$15
Tier 3	Preferred brand-name drugs	$30–$50
Tier 4	Other brand-name drugs	$75–$100+
Tier 5	Specialty drugs	25% coinsurance

Costs can vary by plan; always check your plan's list of covered drugs (formulary).

Real-Life Scenarios

Frank: The Frugal Pharmacist

Frank takes three generic medications. He selects a Part D plan with a $10 monthly premium and a $590 deductible. His total monthly drug cost is under $20.

Marie: Managing Chronic Conditions

Marie requires insulin and a blood thinner. She opts for a plan with comprehensive coverage for her medications. Although her monthly premium is higher, she benefits from the $2,100 out-of-pocket cap, saving her hundreds annually.

🛒 *Shopping Smart for a Part D Plan*

To choose the best Part D plan for your needs:

- List all your current medications and dosages.
- Use the Medicare Plan Finder at Medicare.gov to compare plans.
- Check each plan's list of covered drugs (formulary) to ensure your drugs are covered.
- Consider pharmacy networks; some plans offer better pricing at preferred pharmacies.
- Look for additional benefits like mail-order options or medication therapy management.

✅ My Medicare Checklist: Your Part D Checklist

☐ Do I currently take prescription medications?

☐ Have I compared Part D plans based on my medication needs?

☐ Is my preferred pharmacy in-network for the plan I'm considering?

☐ Do I qualify for Extra Help to assist with Part D costs?

☐ Have I reviewed the plan's formulary for any changes for the upcoming year?

Chapter 8: Extra Help and Savings Programs: Assistance for Tight Budgets

Healthcare costs can be daunting, but Medicare offers programs to ease the financial burden for people with limited income and resources. Let's explore the assistance that was available, including Medicare Savings Programs and Low-Income Subsidies.

▣ *Medicare Savings Programs (MSPs)*

MSPs assist with Medicare Part A and Part B costs. Eligibility and benefits vary:

- **Qualified Medicare Beneficiary (QMB)**: Covers Part A and B premiums, deductibles, coinsurance, and copayments.
- **Specified Low-Income Medicare Beneficiary (SLMB)**: Helps pay Part B premiums.
- **Qualifying Individual (QI)**: Assists with Part B premiums; not available to those on Medicaid.
- **Qualified Disabled and Working Individual (QDWI)**: Pays Part A premiums for certain disabled individuals under 65.

Note: Income and resource limits apply and can vary by state. Contact your state Medicaid office for specific criteria.

✎ *Extra Help (Low-Income Subsidy)*

Extra Help reduces costs for Medicare Part D prescription drug coverage. Benefits include:

- Lower monthly premiums and annual deductibles.
- Reduced copayments for prescriptions.

- No coverage gap or late enrollment penalty.

Eligibility is based on income and resources; limits may vary by state.

Applying for Assistance

To apply for MSPs or Extra Help:

- Contact your state Medicaid office.
- Visit Medicare.gov for information and applications.
- Call Social Security at 1-800-772-1213.

Chapter 9: Navigating Medicare Advantage Plans

So, you've got the basics of Original Medicare down—Part A for hospitals, Part B for doctors—and maybe even a grip on Part D. But what if there were a way to bundle all of that (and maybe even more) into one plan?

Welcome to the world of **Medicare Advantage (Part C)**—where Medicare goes private, and you get choices.

What Is Medicare Advantage?

Medicare Advantage plans (Part C) are offered by private insurance companies that have been approved by Medicare. These plans replace Original Medicare (Parts A + B), but they still keep you in the Medicare program, and they often include extra benefits like:

- Prescription drug coverage (Part D)
- Dental, vision, and hearing insurance
- Gym memberships
- Telehealth services

If you sign up for a Medicare Advantage plan, you still pay your Part B premium, but sometimes Medicare Advantage plans have $0 premiums themselves.

What's in the Package?

Here's what many Medicare Advantage plans (Part C) roll into one:

Included in the Plan	Original Medicare	Medicare Advantage
Part A (hospital)	✓	✓
Part B (doctor/outpatient)	✓	✓
Part D (drug coverage)	✗ (add separately)	✓ (usually included)
Dental, vision, hearing	✗	✓ (varies by plan)
Annual out-of-pocket max	✗	✓

Pros and Cons: Know Before You Choose

👍 **Pros:**

- All-in-one convenience
- Extra benefits beyond Original Medicare (Parts A + B)
- Predictable out-of-pocket limits
- Often lower premiums

👎 **Cons:**

- Limited provider networks (HMO/PPO)
- Referrals may be required
- Plans can change each year
- You may need prior approval for certain services

Real-Life Scenario

Jackie:

Jackie is active, takes minimal meds, and doesn't want to juggle multiple plans. She picks a $0 premium Medicare Advantage plan that includes gym membership, dental, and Part D coverage—all in one. Her only surprise? How easy it was to use.

🛒 How to Shop for a Medicare Advantage Plan

To find a plan that fits your life:

Work with an independent licensed agent/broker who specializes in Medicare for personalized advice.

- ☑ Use Medicare's Plan Finder tool at medicare.gov/plan-compare.
- ☑ Check if your doctors and hospitals are in-network
- ☑ Make sure your prescriptions are covered and what they'll cost.
- ☑ Compare extras like dental, vision, and fitness perks.
- ☑ Look up plan ratings (1–5 stars).

☑ My Medicare Action Plan: Your Medicare Advantage Checklist

- ☐ Do I want drug, dental, and vision coverage all in one plan?
- ☐ Are my doctors/hospitals in-network?
- ☐ What's my annual out-of-pocket max?
- ☐ Am I comfortable with HMO or PPO rules?
- ☐ Do I travel a lot or need nationwide coverage?

Chapter 10: How to Change Plans
(And When You Should)

You picked a Medicare plan, but now you're wondering, *What if I change my mind?* The good news? Medicare isn't a one-and-done situation. Life changes, and so can your coverage. Here's how to switch it up smartly and confidently.

↻ *When Can You Change Medicare Plans?*
Unfortunately, you can't just switch plans whenever you feel like it. But there are specific windows when you can make changes:

1. Annual Enrollment Period (AEP)
October 15 – December 7 every year

- Switch from Original Medicare (Parts A + B) to a Medicare Advantage plan (Part C).
- Switch from one Medicare Advantage plan (Part C) to another.
- Join, drop, or switch prescription drug plans (Part D).

Your adjusted coverage will begin January 1 of the following year.

2. Medicare Advantage Open Enrollment (MAOEP)
January 1 – March 31 every year

- Switch from one Medicare Advantage plan (Part C) to another.
- Drop your Medicare Advantage plan (Part C) and return to Original Medicare (Parts A + B) (with or without a prescription drug plan [Part D])

3. Special Enrollment Periods (SEPs)

You may qualify for a SEP if you:

- Move to a new area.
- Lose current coverage.
- Get Extra Help or Medicaid.
- Enter or leave a nursing home.
- Experience another qualifying life event, such as a natural disaster.
- End work with your employer.

You might want to switch if:

- Your doctor or favorite hospital is no longer in-network.
- Your prescriptions got more expensive—or new ones aren't covered.
- You're traveling more and need broader coverage.
- You want extra benefits your current plan doesn't offer.
- You found a better deal. (Yes, it's allowed to shop around!)

Real-Life Scenario
Ron: The Savvy Switcher

Ron signed up for a Medicare Advantage plan (Part C) with a great gym perk. But after moving to a different state, he found none of his doctors were in-network. During the Annual Enrollment Period (AEP), he switched to a new Advantage plan tailored to his new ZIP code—and even found a plan with better dental benefits.

How to Make the Switch

Making changes is easier than you think. Here's how.

- ☐ Review your current plan's Annual Notice of Change (ANOC), which is mailed every September
- ☐ Compare plans at Medicare.gov. Look for changes in costs, coverage, and drug lists.
- ☐ Call 1-800-MEDICARE or use the Plan Finder tool at https://www.medicare.gov to enroll.

- ☐ Work with a licensed independent agent/broker who specializes in Medicare for personalized advice.
- ☐ Pro tip: Don't cancel your old plan until the new one is confirmed.

☑ My Medicare Action Plan: Should I Change My Medicare Plan?

☐ Have my health or medication needs changed?
☐ Is my plan getting more expensive or restrictive?
☐ Am I eligible for Extra Help or Medicaid now?
☐ Did I move or retire recently?
☐ Have I checked new plans for better coverage?

Chapter 11: Avoiding Common Medicare Mistakes (So You Don't Learn the Hard Way!)

Medicare is powerful, but it's also packed with rules, timelines, and traps that missing can cost you—big time. Whether you're brand new or already enrolled, avoiding these common mistakes can save you thousands of dollars—and a whole lot of headaches.

Let's break them down and fix them before they happen.

Mistake #1: Missing Your Initial Enrollment Period (IEP)
Your Initial Enrollment Period (IEP) is a seven-month window:

- Three months *before* the month you turn 65
- Your birthday month
- Three months *after*

If you miss that window and don't have other creditable coverage (like from an employer), you could:

- Pay late penalties—for life
- Wait months for your coverage to kick in

💡 **Fix**: Even if you're still working, confirm that your employer coverage is creditable. If not, enroll in Medicare on time.

Mistake #2: Thinking Medicare Is Free
Medicare is amazing, but it's not free.
Here's what you'll likely pay in 2026.

Medicare Part	Monthly Premium (2026)	Notes
Part A	$0 (if you paid taxes ≥10 years)	Could pay up to $565 / month if less years worked(2026)
Part B	$202.90 (income-based)	May be higher for high earners IRMAA
Part D	Varies by plan (~$30–$50 a month avg)	Late penalties apply if you delay
Medigap	Varies by state, age, and plan	Typically, $100–$250/month
Part C (Advantage)	$0–$100+	Many offer $0 premiums

💡**Fix:** Build your Medicare costs into your retirement budget—including copays and deductibles.

Mistake #3: Delaying Part D Because "I Don't Take Meds"

Even if you're not on prescriptions now, delaying Part D can trigger a lifetime late penalty—1% of the national base premium per month delayed.

In 2026, that base premium is $34.50, so a 12-month delay = 10% penalty added monthly—forever.

💡**Fix:** Enroll in the lowest-cost Part D plan during your IEP to avoid future penalties.

Mistake #4: Assuming All Doctors Accept Medicare Advantage

Not all providers take all plans—and networks change!

If your doctor or hospital isn't in your Medicare Advantage plan's network, you could:

- Pay more out-of-pocket
- Be denied coverage

💡**Fix:** Before enrolling (and every fall), confirm that your providers are in-network. Plans can change yearly.

Mistake #5: Ignoring Travel and Coverage Gaps

Love to travel? Spend winters in Florida? Medicare Advantage plans (Part C) often restrict you to local networks.

Fix: If you're a traveler or snowbird, consider:

- Original Medicare + Medigap (offers nationwide coverage)
- A PPO Advantage plan with out-of-network benefits
- Plans with foreign travel emergency care

Mistake #6: Choosing Based Only on Premiums

A $0 premium sounds great—until you get hit with:

- $50 copays per doctor visit
- $200 hospital per day stays
- $500 in drug costs

Fix: Look at the full picture:
- Monthly premium
- Out-of-pocket maximum
- Prescription costs
- Your typical care needs

Mistake #7: Never Reviewing Your Coverage

Plans change. Drugs move tiers. Providers and hospitals drop out of network. Costs go up.

Fix: Use the Annual Enrollment Period (Oct 15 – Dec 7) to:

- Re-evaluate your needs.
- Compare plans at Medicare.gov/plan, or reach out to your agent.
- Switch to better coverage if needed.

Real-Life Scenario
Lisa: The Problem Fixer

Lisa had a prescription drug plan (Part D) for years. One fall, she noticed a medication that she was on was moved to a non-preferred tier, and her cost jumped from $35 to $160 per month. After comparing plans during the Annual Enrollment

Period (AEP), she switched and brought it back down to \$35/month with a \$0 deductible.

Moral of the story? Check every year.

☑ My Medicare Action Plan: 2026 Medicare Mistake Prevention Checklist

☐ Know your enrollment periods (IEP, AEP, SEP)

☐ Enroll in Part B and D on time—even if you feel healthy!

☐ Check if your employer coverage is "creditable."

☐ Compare total costs—not just premiums.

☐ Review plan changes annually, including drug lists, networks, and costs.

☐ Ask for help. Free State Health Insurance Assistance program counselors (SHIP) or licensed agents are a call away.

Chapter 12: Working Past 65? Here's What You Need to Know

Retiring at 65 isn't the rule anymore. Whether you're working full-time, part-time, or consulting on your own terms, Medicare and job-based coverage need to play nice. Let's walk through how to do it *right*—without overpaying or missing deadlines.

Do You Need to Sign Up for Medicare at 65?
It depends on your work situation *and* your employer's size. Here's the breakdown.

Employer Size	Still Working at 65?	Do You *Need* to Enroll in Medicare?
Less than 20 employees	☑ Yes	✔ Enroll in Medicare at 65 because your employer plan may not be primary.
20 or more employees	☑ Yes	✘ Optional because employer coverage usually stays primary.
Self-employed	☑ Yes	✔ Enroll in Medicare unless you have other creditable coverage.

☑ **Creditable coverage** means your job-based insurance is as good as Medicare. If it's not, you *must* enroll to avoid penalties.

Working and Medicare: Your Coverage Combo Options
Option A: Keep Employer Insurance + Enroll in Medicare A (Only)

This is common because:

- Part A is usually free.
- It acts as *secondary insurance*, helping cover hospital bills.

Medicare Part	Sign Up?	Why?
Part A	✔ Yes	It's free and can fill in gaps from employer plan.
Part B	✘ No	Skip if your employer insurance is creditable.
Part D	✘ No	Only enroll if you don't have drug coverage at work.

Option B: Drop Employer Plan and Go Full Medicare
This works if:

- Your work coverage is expensive.
- You're eligible for a good Medicare Advantage plan (Part C) or Medigap plan.

Coverage Option	Typical Monthly Cost (2025)	Notes
Part A (hospital)	$0 (if qualified)	Free for most
Part B (doctor)	$202.90	Income-based
Part D (drug)	$30–$50 avg	Compare plans
Medigap or Advantage	$0–$100+	Varies by plan and location

⚠ *What Happens If You Wait Too Long?*
If you **don't have creditable coverage** and delay Part B or D:

- You might have to wait months for coverage to start.
- You'll face a late enrollment penalty for life. 2025 Late Enrollment Penalties:

- **Part B**: 10% penalty *for each full year you delay*
- **Part D**: 1% of the national base premium ($34.50/ month in 2026) *for each month delayed*
- Example: Delay Part D for 12 months = 10% extra per month *forever*.

☑ My Medicare Action Plan: If You're Working Past 65 Checklist

☐ How many employees does your employer have?
☐ Is your current insurance considered "creditable"?
☐ Should you enroll in Medicare Part A now if it's free?
☐ Do you need Part B or D—or can you delay without penalty?
☐ When you retire, do you know how to trigger a Special Enrollment Period (SEP)?

Special Enrollment Period (SEP) for Part B and D

When you leave your job (or lose coverage), you have:

- Eight months to enroll in Part B without penalty.
- 63 days to sign up for a prescription drug plan (Part D).

Use CMS Form 40B and CMS-L564 to enroll in Medicare after age 65 with no penalties.

Real-Life Scenario
Charles: The Angry Assumer

Charles is 66 and works for a company with 15 employees. He assumed he didn't need to sign up for Medicare. After a hospital visit, he learned his employer's insurance wasn't primary—and Medicare should've been. He had to pay the bill *and* got hit with a Part B penalty.

Moral of the story? Know the rules.

Chapter 13: Getting the Most from Your Medicare Coverage

🎁 Perks, Preventive Care, and Powerful Freebies You Might Be Missing

You've got Medicare—great! But did you know it offers more than just doctor visits and hospital stays? You might be leaving valuable services (and even some fun stuff) on the table.

Let's unlock the full value of your Medicare coverage—because it's time to get everything you've earned.

🩺 *1. Preventive Services: Catch It Before It Becomes a Problem*

Medicare covers a ton of **free preventive services** to keep you healthy. The following services are covered at *no cost* to you.

Service	Cost	Frequency
Annual wellness visit	$0	Once every 12 months
Mammogram	$0	Every 12 months (women 40+)
Colorectal cancer screening	$0	Every 10 years (or more often if high-risk)
Flu shot	$0	Every flu season
COVID-19 vaccine	$0	As recommended
Diabetes screenings	$0	If you're at risk
Depression screening	$0	Once a year, in a primary care setting

Pro Tip: Your first year on Medicare includes a "Welcome to Medicare" visit with your primary care physician. That sets the foundation for personalized care.

2. Fitness and Wellness Benefits (Especially with Advantage Plans)

If you have a Medicare Advantage plan (Part C), chances are you have free or discounted wellness perks. Check your plan booklet or portal because benefits vary by carrier and region.

Benefit	What You Get
SilverSneakers or Renew Active	Free gym memberships, fitness classes, online workouts
Nutrition coaching	Some plans offer one-on-one dietitian support
Mental health resources	Counseling, therapy, or virtual support tools
Over-the-counter (OTC) allowance	$25–$100/month for vitamins, bandages, cold meds & more

3. Travel Coverage: Know Before You Go

Original Medicare doesn't cover most care outside the United States, but some Medigap policies (like Plans C, D, F, G, M, and N) do.

Travel Situation	What Covers It?
U.S. domestic travel	All Medicare plans (check network if Advantage)
International emergencies	Some Medigap plans
Routine foreign care	Not covered under Original Medicare

✈ Planning to travel abroad? Check your Medigap or Advantage plan to see what's included—or consider purchasing short-term travel medical insurance.

Real-Life Scenario
Rosa: The Super Saver
Rosa is 67 and didn't realize her Medicare Advantage plan (Part C) gave her:

- $100 over-the-counter card each quarter
- Free dental cleanings
- SilverSneakers access at her local gym

She was paying for a private fitness class and buying her vitamins out-of-pocket—until she checked her benefits portal and started using her plan to the fullest. Now she's saving more than $800 each year!

☑ My Medicare Action Plan: Medicare Maximizer Checklist

☐ Schedule your free annual wellness visit.
☐ Use your plan's fitness and OTC benefits.
☐ Ask about covered dental, vision, and hearing services.
☐ Use telehealth when appropriate
☐ Review travel coverage before your next trip
☐ Log in to your Medicare plan account. There's gold in there!

Pro Tip: If you're unsure what your plan covers, call customer service or talk to a licensed broker/agent who specializes in Medicare. They can help you find hidden perks you're already paying for.

Chapter 14: Help! What to Do When Something Goes Wrong (Claims, Denials, and Appeals)

Let's be real—insurance can get messy. Maybe your bill looks too high, your service wasn't covered, or a claim was flat-out denied. You're not alone.

This chapter is your Medicare problem-solving toolkit, complete with real-life scenarios, steps to fix things, and a few insider tips to keep your cool when the paperwork piles up.

Common Medicare Problems (And What They Really Mean)

Situation	What's Going On	What You Can Do
Medicare denied a service	It may not be "medically necessary" (in their eyes)	File an appeal with doctor's support
You got a surprise bill	You might've seen an out-of-network provider	Check your plan's coverage & call the provider
A prescription isn't covered	It may not be on your drug plan's formulary	Request an exception or change plans during the annual enrollment period
A claim was rejected	Info might be wrong or missing	Contact your provider & Medicare to fix it

Step-by-Step: How to Appeal a Medicare Denial

If you've received a "Medicare Summary Notice" (MSN) or a denial letter, don't panic. Here's your action plan.

Step 1: Review the MSN or Explanation of Benefits (EOB)

- This is your itemized bill from Medicare or your plan
- Look for codes or explanations of the denial

Step 2: Submit a Written Appeal

- You have 120 days from the date on your MSN
- Fill out the appeal form on the back of the notice *or* write a letter
- Include: Your name, Medicare number, denied service, reason for appeal, and supporting medical documents

Mail it to the address listed on the notice or your Medicare Advantage/Part D plan provider.

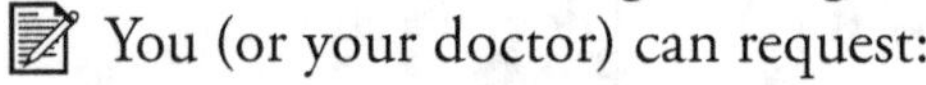 Step 3: Ask Your Doctor to Help

A letter from your physician explaining why the service is medically necessary can significantly improve your chances.

What If It's a Drug That's Denied?

For Medicare Part D drug coverage issues:

You (or your doctor) can request:

- Formulary exceptions
- Tiering exceptions
- Prior authorization

Your plan must respond within **72 hours** for standard requests or **24 hours** for expedited cases.

Real-Life Scenario

Don

Don had back surgery and got hit with a $1,600 bill. Medicare denied a key part of the claim, saying it wasn't necessary. Don worked with his surgeon to write a detailed appeal letter.

Three weeks later: the denial was reversed, and Medicare paid the claim in full. Moral: If it feels wrong, speak up.

☎ Who to Call When You Need Backup

📞 Help Resource	💬 What They Do	📍 Contact
1-800-MEDICARE	General questions, billing issues	Available 24/7
SHIP Counselor	Free, local help with claims and appeals	Find yours include link?
State Ombudsman	Help with Medicare Advantage & Part D disputes	Through your state department of aging
Your Plan's Customer Service	First stop for Advantage or Part D issues	Phone number on back of your card

☑ My Medicare Action Plan: Medicare Dispute Survival Checklist

☐ Double-check your MSN or Explanation of Benefits
☐ Contact the provider to fix any errors
☐ Write or file a timely appeal
☐ Get written support from your doctor
☐ Follow up regularly
☐ Get help from SHIP independent agent or 1-800-MEDICARE if stuck

📖 Know Your Rights

- You have the right to a fair appeal process
- You have the right to explanations in writing
- You have the right to get help at no cost

Chapter 15: Medicare and Medicaid — Can You Have Both? (And How It Works)

🤝 *The Dual Eligibility Guide*

If you're low-income and eligible for Medicare, you might also qualify for Medicaid—a state-run program that helps pay for health costs. Together, they can provide powerful coverage. Let's break it all down—because if you're eligible for both, you deserve to get every benefit without the red tape headache.

Medicare vs. Medicaid — What's the Difference?

Program	Who It's For	What It Covers	Who Runs It
Medicare	Age 65+ or disabled	Hospital, medical, drug coverage	Federal government
Medicaid	Low-income individuals/ families	Medical + long-term care	State governments (varies by state)
Dual Eligible	Low income + age 65+/ disabled	Both Medicare + Medicaid benefits	Jointly managed

Are You Dual Eligible?

You may qualify for both if:

You're eligible for Medicare.

You meet income and asset limits in your state.

Dual Eligibility Income Limits (Estimates)

Household Size	Monthly Income Limit (Full Medicaid)	Monthly Income Limit (Partial Help)
1 person	~$1,255/month	Up to ~$1,700/month
2 people	~$1,704/month	Up to ~$2,300/month

💰 **Assets** (like savings): Typically must be under ~$9,430 for an individual or ~$14,130 for a couple (limits vary by state).

🔑 **Pro Tip:** Check with your state Medicaid office or SHIP counselor to get your specific local numbers.

What Benefits Do You Get If You Have Both?

If you're dual eligible, your Medicaid helps pay for what Medicare doesn't, including:

- **Part B premium** (covered for most duals)
- **Deductibles and copays**
- **Long-term care** services (like nursing homes)
- **Dental, vision, and hearing** (depending on state)
- **Transportation to medical appointments**

💡 You may also qualify for a **Special Needs Plan (SNP)** designed for dual-eligible individuals.

Real-Life Scenario
Angela

Angela is 68, lives alone, and gets Social Security. Her income is $1,200/month, and she has minimal savings. She qualifies for full Medicaid + Medicare and gets:

- **$0 monthly premium**
- **$0 drug copays**
- **Free dental cleanings**
- **Assistance with transportation to her doctor**

Angela didn't even know she qualified—until she talked to a SHIP counselor. Now she's saving thousands a year.

Dual Eligible Special Needs Plans (D-SNPs)
A D-SNP is a **Medicare Advantage plan made for people with both Medicare & Medicaid**.
Benefits may include:

- Extra dental, vision, and hearing coverage
- Healthy food cards
- Care coordination (someone to help manage your doctors and meds)
- $0 copays for many services

Want help finding a D-SNP? Medicare's Plan Finder at Medicare.gov has a tool for that or seek out a local knowledgeable independent agent / broker.

✅ My Medicare Action Plan: If You Think You Might Be Dual Eligible Checklist

☐ Check your income & asset levels
☐ Apply for Medicaid through your state website or office
☐ Ask about a Medicare Savings Program (MSP)
☐ Explore D-SNPs in your area
☐ Get free help from a SHIP counselor

Where to Get Help

Resource	What They Do
SHIP (State Health Insurance Assistance Program)	Free local counseling
Your state Medicaid Office	Handles applications & questions
1-800-MEDICARE	Federal Medicare assistance
Social Security	Helps with Medicare Savings Program applications

Chapter 16: Medicare Scams and Fraud: How to Spot (and Stop) Them

Stay sharp. Stay safe. This is your Medicare defense manual. You've worked hard for your Medicare benefits. Don't let scammers cash in on them. Fraud is real, and it's more common than you think.

What Counts as Medicare Fraud?

What It Is	Examples
Billing for services not provided	You're charged for a test or visit you never had.
Double billing	The same service is billed twice.
Fake providers	Someone poses as a doctor or Medicare rep.
Unnecessary services	Getting billed for extra tests or treatments you didn't need.
Stolen Medicare numbers	Your Medicare card is used by someone else.

Common Medicare Scams to Watch For

1. "Free" medical equipment calls

"You qualify for a back brace at no cost!" They bill Medicare for hundreds of dollars using your info. It might be a way for the "company" to get your Medicare number and bill fraudulent charges.

2. Imposter phone calls

"This is Medicare. We need to verify your number." Medicare will *never* call you asking for your number.

3. Fake health fairs or screenings

You sign up for a service, give your Medicare info, and it gets misused.

4. "New Medicare card" scam

"You need a new plastic Medicare card—just confirm your number."

Nope. Medicare cards don't expire, and you don't need to pay for replacements.

How to Protect Yourself

1. Review your Medicare Summary Notice (MSN).

It shows everything Medicare was billed on your behalf.
Look for charges you don't recognize—especially things you didn't receive.

2. Don't share your Medicare number.

Treat it like your Social Security or credit card number. Only share it with:

- Your doctor or pharmacist.
- Medicare itself (1-800-MEDICARE).
- Licensed insurance agents you trust.

3. Hang up on unsolicited calls.

If someone calls out of the blue asking for your Medicare number, hang up. Then report it to the Federal Trade Commission (FTC).

How to Report Medicare Fraud

If you suspect something shady, don't wait. Report it. You could help protect others, and you even get back overcharged funds.

Where to Report	What They Do
1-800-MEDICARE	Official reporting line
OIG hotline	Office of Inspector General: 1-800-HHS-TIPS
SMP (Senior Medicare Patrol)	Helps educate and report scams locally: smpresource.org

Pro Tip: If you ever unwittingly give your Medicare number to a scammer, you're not stuck. Call 1-800-MEDICARE and ask them to monitor your account or even issue a new card.

Real-Life Scenario
Calvin: The Unwitting Victim
Calvin got a call about a "free knee brace." They only needed his Medicare number. A few weeks later, he noticed a $486 charge for medical supplies he never received.

He called **1-800-MEDICARE**, reported the fraud, and the charge was removed. His number was flagged for extra monitoring. Crisis averted.

✔ My Medicare Action Plan: Fraud Prevention Checklist
☐ Keep your Medicare card in a safe place.
☐ Shred old Medicare documents.
☐ Watch for unknown charges on MSNs.
☐ Never give your number over the phone.
☐ Report anything suspicious right away.

Chapter 17: The Medicare Glossary: Speak the Language Like a Pro

Medicare is packed with acronyms and terms that can feel like another language. This glossary will keep you from getting lost in the alphabet soup. Bookmark it, highlight it, dog-ear it. It's your not-so-secret decoder ring for Medicare.

🏥 Core Medicare Terms

- **Medicare Part A**: Hospital insurance. Covers inpatient stays, skilled nursing, hospice, and some home health care.
- **Medicare Part B**: Medical insurance. Covers doctor visits, outpatient care, preventive services, and durable medical equipment.
- **Medicare Part C (Medicare Advantage)**: A private plan option that replaces Original Medicare, often bundling Part A, B, and D plus extras like dental and vision.
- **Medicare Part D**: Prescription drug coverage. Sold as stand-alone plans or built into Advantage plans.

💰 Cost-Related Terms

- **Premium**: What you pay monthly to have coverage
- **Deductible**: What you pay before Medicare or your plan kicks in
- **Copay**: Fixed dollar amount you pay for a service (like $20 for a doctor visit)
- **Coinsurance**: A percentage you pay (like 20% of a bill)

- **Out-of-pocket maximum**: The most you'll pay in a year for covered services (applies to Advantage plans, not Original Medicare)

📅 Enrollment Terms

- **Initial Enrollment Period (IEP)**: Your seven-month window when you first become eligible for Medicare at 65
- **General Enrollment Period (GEP)**: January 1–March 31 each year if you missed signing up initially
- **Special Enrollment Period (SEP)**: Timeframes outside the usual windows, triggered by life events like losing employer coverage
- **Annual Enrollment Period (AEP)**: October 15–December 7: The big window to change or switch plans
- **Open Enrollment Period (OEP)**: January 1–March 31 for Medicare Advantage members to switch or go back to Original Medicare

📄 Plan Terms

- **Formulary**: The list of drugs covered by your Part D or Advantage plan
- **Network**: The doctors, hospitals, and providers contracted with your plan
- **Prior Authorization**: Approval needed before your plan covers certain services or medications
- **Medigap (supplemental insurance)**: Private insurance that helps pay the gaps (deductibles, copays, coinsurance) in Original Medicare

Chapter 18: Putting It All Together: Your Medicare Action Plan

You've made it through the Medicare maze! Congratulations! By now, you've learned the parts, plans, costs, and choices. But knowledge only matters if you put it into action. This chapter is your roadmap: a step-by-step checklist to help you feel confident as you make your Medicare decisions.

Step 1: Know Your Timeline

- **Turning 65 soon?** Mark your seven-month Initial Enrollment Period (three months before, the month of, and three months after your birthday).
- **Still working past 65?** Coordinate with your employer coverage to avoid late penalties.
- **Already on Medicare?** Use the Annual Enrollment Period (Oct. 15–Dec. 7) to review and make changes.

✔ *Action item: Write your enrollment dates on your calendar.*

Step 2: Get Real About Your Budget

- Calculate how much you can comfortably spend each month on premiums.
- Think about your typical healthcare needs: Do you visit the doctor often? Take regular prescriptions?
- Remember to factor in deductibles, copays, and coinsurance—not just premiums.

✔ *Action item: Use a Medicare cost calculator (like medicare. gov) to compare estimated expenses.*

🏥 *Step 3: Choose Your Coverage Path*

- **Original Medicare + Medigap + Part D** → Great for flexibility, travel, and fewer surprise bills.
- **Medicare Advantage (Part C)** → Great if you like bundled coverage, lower premiums, and extra perks like dental and vision.

✅ *Action item: Make a pros/cons list that matches your lifestyle.*

💊 *Step 4: Check Your Prescriptions*

Drug coverage is where costs sneak up.

- Review plan formularies carefully.
- Double-check copay tiers and preferred pharmacies.
- Look into Extra Help if your prescription costs strain your budget.

✅ *Action item: List your medications and compare plan costs for each.*

⚕️ *Step 5: Confirm Your Doctors & Hospitals*

Don't assume your providers are covered. *Networks matter.*

- Search for your doctors in plan directories.
- If you travel often, look for plans with broader networks.

✅ *Action item: Call your doctor's office to confirm they accept your plan.*

🛡️ *Step 6: Protect Yourself from Mistakes*

- Watch out for late enrollment penalties.
- Review your plan every year—don't just auto-renew.
- Be alert for scams: Medicare will never call asking for payment over the phone.

✅ *Action item: Keep a Medicare file folder with copies of your notices, bills, and plan info.*

✅ **My Medicare Action Plan: Success Checklist**

- ☐ I know my enrollment dates.
- ☐ I've set a budget for premiums and out-of-pocket costs.

- ☐ I've chosen between Original Medicare + Medigap or Medicare Advantage.
- ☐ My prescriptions are covered at a fair cost.
- ☐ My doctors and hospitals are in-network.
- ☐ I understand my annual review and enrollment options.

✨ *Final Thoughts*

Medicare isn't one-size-fits-all. It's about finding what fits *you*. The key is to stay proactive, ask questions, and review your choices each year. With this book, you're no longer just hoping for the best. You're making informed, confident decisions.

Congratulations, you're officially ready to take charge of your Medicare journey! 🚀

MEDICARE ROADMAP

1 KNOW YOUR TIMELINE
Mark your enrollment dates and annual review periods

2 GET REAL ABOUT YOUR BUDGET
Calculate how much you can afford for premiums and out-of-pocket costs

3 CHOOSE YOUR COVERAGE PATH
Decide between Original Medicare or Medicare Advantage

4 CHECK YOUR PRESCRIPTIONS
Compare drug coverage and find plans that fit your needs

5 CONFIRM YOUR DOCTORS
Verify that your providers are in-network for your plan

6 PROTECT YOURSELF
Be aware of potential penalties

Acknowledgments

This book took a long time in the making. The idea sat with me for almost five years, but I wanted to make it a reality! I want to thank Stephanie, my wife, whose focus and inspiration inspired me to finish this project and my children, Andrew, Madeline, Michael and Sean. I also want to thank my mom, Barbara Stark, who is a super Medicare beneficiary in her own right!

Special thanks goes to the National Association of Benefit Insurance professionals and the Medicare Advisory Board. Their advocacy on behalf of Medicare beneficiaries is unmatched.

Thanks also to Desmond Slattery, whose words ring true to this day: "If you already know a little about insurance you already know more than almost everyone else."

About the Author

Toby Stark is the founder of Stark Associates Insurance Agency in Red Bank, New Jersey. The agency specializes in Medicare planning, group and individual benefits, long-term care and disability benefits. Toby has been an active member of National Association of Benefit Insurance Professionals (NABIP) since 2009 and has served as president of the New Jersey Association of Benefit Insurance Professionals (NJABIP) from 2016 to 2017.

He also serves on the NJABIP state legislative affairs committee. In this role, Toby meets with legislators on the viewpoints of the association. The regular meetings serve as an education so that these regulators have a better understanding of the large scope of impact and how it could affect their constituents the voting Medicare beneficiary.

Toby is also currently serving on the Medicare Advisory Board for NABIP. He also serves on the board of directors of the Monmouth—Ocean Development Council promoting business advocacy in the bi-county area in his home state New Jersey.

For More Information

Website: www.stark-associates.com
Phone: 866-955-8224 toll free or 732-747-0411
Or just type Toby Stark Medicare in your search engine.
To book a speaking engagement, please reach out to me at toby@stark-associates.com.